the house on the hill: a poetry collection

Annie Deering

Presentation by *BookLeaf Publishing*

Web: www.bookleafpub.com

E-mail: info@bookleafpub.com

ISBN: 9789357446440

First edition 2022

DEDICATION

for Momma - "I carry you in my heart."

ACKNOWLEDGE MENT

Thank you to all of my loved ones for the continuous support of both my art and my wellbeing, which are commonly intertwined;
to my pets for keeping me company on the nights I spend creating;
to BookLeaf, for this accessible publishing opportunity;
to the Earth that holds us.
I am current occupying and writing on Oneida and Haudenosaunee land.

PREFACE

Hello there! Welcome to a selection of pieces that I've been working on this month. I invite you to communicate with the pieces, to let them resonate with you, or to leave them behind if they do not serve you. This book is for you and for me.

mountain man

i drive down the mountain listening to soul
music.
"this will be / an everlasting love".
the passenger seat is empty, but my pup sticks
her head out the back window.
the breeze is cool, and the leaves are changing.
autumn peeks from behind a corner,
enticing you into their annual game of hide and
seek.
i am here, mustard yellow, golden corn.
and you wonder why i always wear yellow.

probably

sometimes, no answer is an answer

sorry that you weren't having fun

i don't know when to stop
i don't know how to get out
i don't know - but it would probably feel bad
either way.

third generation

here are some places that i daydream about
spending time:

california, where even the baby redwoods are
thicker than my thigh;

maine, where the coast that my mom had always
wanted to drive resides;

tennessee, to see my freckle-faced, red-haired
niece who's always up to mischief;

thailand, to taste the noodles that make my
friends feel at home;

india, to see the dance that my friend has learned
for seven years, practicing from california to
singapore;

holland, where my grandfather never stepped, as
his family emigrated to the US for a better life,
where i dreamed my mother would step.

and once more, for them, for me, i wake up to
dream.

untitled

i've been having nightmares
bad roommate, nothing is clean, assignments are
late
i vomit blood onto the stage in my high school
theatre, rushing to rehearsal
i'm late
i'm late
i'm bleeding, but i'm late
i don't know the dance
i'm the last in the line and i fumble. they know.
has it been a few hours? a few days?
my mom, eyes glazed, acting unlike herself.
"please, take care of your only child!"
no response.
my sister hangs off the back deck, smiling.
she calls me by the wrong name. a name i don't
like.
i respond.

artistic feedback loop

step one: you need to post art to sell art. get online and maintain your social media presence.

step two: get screen fatigue and compare yourself to other artists.

step three: feel uninspired. get creative block.

step four: begin doom scrolling to "just relax".

step five: feel the pressure. just make something already.

step six: return to social media before you're ready, unless you wanna get back to that 9 to 5! chop chop!

rinse and repeat.

desire

I WANT TO CREATE THINGS THAT I LOVE.
I WANT OTHER PEOPLE TO LOVE THEM
TOO.
I WANT MY ART TO BE ACCESSIBLE TO
OTHERS.
I WANT TO EARN A LIVING FROM MY
ART.
I WANT MY JOB TO BE ACCESSIBLE TO
ME.
I WANT TO FEEL MORE JOY.

lover

you won't hold me, but you won't let me go

What would you tell your inner child?

i pause. we are near the end of the session, but i begin to cry.
she tells me it's okay to cry. i know it is; i don't try to stop.

i am speaking through the hot salt on my face, "i wouldn't want to lie to them."

"it gets better, but it still hurts.

i'd want to hold them, to take away all of the hurt and pain and confusion that they were feeling.
there was so much that wasn't her fault.

you can be a kid for as long as you like. forever, even.

you will be loved. you already are.

you will need help, and that does not make you
weak or bad, although sometimes you will be
both.

you will be held."

Alex

she told me good morning
about her job,
her days,
her dog.
she said that she was proud of me after every
therapy session,
and when she was sad, she'd ask to see things
i'd made.
she told me she'd like to see me,
and i haven't seen her since.

morning musings

i took myself to coffee
i had an empty front seat
i thought i would be lonely,
but i'm not lonely with me

Bear

on days that i wake up and can't wipe the haze
out of my eyes,
i let my dog out the back door.
the sun comes through the trees. my feet are wet
with dew.
the light is soft and warm against the cold
morning air.

she tears across the lawn and into the woods.

the leaves and twigs crack underfoot as she
tromps through the fields to the creek,
wading in to her ankles, beginning to drink.

after a few moments, she runs back to me and
looks up.
an invitation to begin again.

lunar tune

when i was a child, i was taught about the sky

told about the planets and the stars, i started
learning why.

they'd say, "every night, the sun dies to let the
moon breathe".

even as a child, i did not believe;

i said, "why should the sun have to die just for
the moon to dream?"
"why smother yourself for someone else to
breathe?"

it's not as easy or as sweet as the stories make it
seem,
but we can write our own if that is what we need

5 things i'm still learning

i am not better or worse than anyone else.

i do not owe anyone anything.

i should not take criticism from anyone that i would not take advice from.

i don't have to rush to feel better every time i feel bad.

some of what i do can be for others, but i need to do for me as well.

affirmations

I am whole as I am.
I am enough.
I am not too much.
I am worthy.
I want to give and receive love.
I will live as kindly as possible.
I am whole as I am.

cardboard box

this past week, my mom came home in a US
Postal Service box;
i held her hesitantly, turning the box in my
hands.
i'd never thought to buy an urn; what kind
would she even have wanted?

i texted a friend with a warm heart that i can feel
all of the way from new york to alaska.
her dad had left his earthly form when she was
young,
and she told me about where she kept her special
cardboard box;
in a place that she could always yell to him.

i rest easier knowing that she's there, safe, on the
shelf in my art studio; a welcome participant.
i rest easier knowing that i have time to lay her
to rest, regardless of her vessel.
i rest easier knowing that sometimes our most
painful moments can help others feel even a
little less alone.

why do you think we fell in love so fast?

the text popped up on my phone. i smiled.
"okay, it's dorky," i began. "but i believe in
soulmates. i don't think that we have just one
necessarily, and i think that we have platonic
ones as well, but i think that some people in our
lives are kind of like kindred spirits."
another text. "BOOOOOO."
another. a heart.
i continued, "the people that understand us that
we understand too; and i think that we were both
open and honest about what we were looking
for. we weren't sure, but we were falling in
love."
"i was just so enamored with you. i still am."
"sometimes you meet folks and wanna date them
for a while and cherish that time together, and
sometimes that's also true, but you wanna keep
learning and growing and going through life
with them. those folks are way fewer and far
between. so yeah, i don't think that we really

had a choice about falling in love. you can't pick your feelings, but you can choose to nurture them."

for my mother annie
- revisited

i shut my eyes tight, like a child awaiting a
surprise,
and dream myself to the heavy storm door
at the front of our home.

i stand carefully atop the second brick step that
i'd skinned my knees on some years before.
the air tastes fresh; the trees and mountains share
their bounty.
i have a key, but i like to knock.

your voice. moments later, the door swings open
and your face is always the same:
Warm. Familiar. Welcome.
a bit thinner than usual, but as beautiful as ever.
my force of nature.

out pour the smells of you,
the haze of incense burning,
the blaze of the wood stove to warm your bones,
floating, heavy as wet snow, light as linen.

i have always believed in our tiny house,
but in your arms, i am home.

-

years later, my toes still press against cold
hardwood when i wake. your spirit is here, in the
celestial tiles, the clothesline, the runoff in the
creek. in your arms, i was home. now, you hold
me with afternoons on the back deck and
squeaky dutch stairs. i am home.

for Ollie

they touch recovery
a warm, possible gift.
choice, nourished by balance.
if love grows weary,
cherish your heart.
accept it as whole.

www.ingramcontent.com/pod-product-compliance
Lightning Source LLC
LaVergne TN
LVHW021345200726

843509LV00014B/2683